ANCIENT HISTORY

ANITA GANERI

Published 2008 by
A & C Black Publishers Ltd.
38 Soho Square, London, W1D 3HB
www.acblack.com

Hardback ISBN 978-1-4081-0409-5

Paperback ISBN 978-1-4081-1093-5

Every effort has been made to trace copyright holders and to obtain their permission for use
of copyright material. The authors and publishers would be pleased to rectify any error or
omission in future editions.

This book is produced using paper that is made from wood grown in managed, sustainable forests.
It is natural, renewable and recyclable. The logging and manufacturing processes conform to the
environmental regulations of the country of origin.

Printed and bound in China by WKT.

All the internet addresses given in this book were correct at the time of going to press.
The author and publishers regret any inconvenience caused if addresses have changed
or sites have ceased to exist, but can accept no responsibility for any such changes.

Acknowledgements
The publishers would like to thank the following for their kind permission to
reproduce their photographs:
Cover image: Ruggero Vaini/CORBIS Pages: 4 Ancient Art & Architecture Collection; Ancient Art
& Architecture Collection; 5 Ronald Sheridan/Ancient Art & Architecture Collection; 6 Ancient Art
& Architecture Collection; 8 Ronald Sheridan/Ancient Art & Architecture Collection; 9 Gianni Dagli
Orti/CORBIS; 10 Prisma/Ancient Art & Architecture Collection; 11 Ronald Sheridan/Ancient Art &
Architecture Collection; 12 Ancient Art & Architecture Collection; 13 John P.Stevens/Ancient Art &
Architecture Collection; 14 Sheridan/Ancient Art & Architecture Collection; 15 Ronald
Sheridan/Ancient Art & Architecture Collection; 16 Ancient Art & Architecture Collection; 17
Ancient Art & Architecture Collection; C.M.Dixon/Ancient Art & Architecture Collection; 18 Gianni
Dagli Orti/CORBIS; 19 C M Dixon/Ancient Art & Architecture Collection; 20 Charles
O'Rear/CORBIS; 21 Ronald Sheridan/Ancient Art & Architecture Collection; 22 Araldo de
Luca/CORBIS; 23 Bettmann/CORBIS; 24 Ronald Sheridan/Ancient Art & Architecture Collection; 25
Gianni Dagli Orti/CORBIS; 26 Sandro Vannini/CORBIS; 27 Bettmann/CORBIS; 28 Ancient Art &
Architecture Collection; 29 Araldo de Luca/CORBIS; 31 G.T.Garvey/Ancient Art & Architecture
Collection; 32 Araldo de Luca/CORBIS; 33 Richard T. Nowitz/CORBIS; 34 Prisma/Ancient
Art&Architecture Collection; 35 Bettmann/CORBIS; 36 Uniphoto Japan/Ancient Art & Architecture
Collection; 37 Dr. S. Coyne/ Ancient Art & Architecture Collection; 38 Uniphoto/AAA Collection;
39 Uniphoto Press Japan/Ancient Art & Architecture Collection; 40 Uniphoto/AAA Collection; 41 A.
P. Maudslay; 42 Aurora/Getty Images; Craig Lovell/CORBIS; 44 Codex Mendoza; 45 The Art
Archive/Corbis.

Contents

Gilgamesh

A legendary king of Sumer in **Mesopotamia** (modern-day Iraq), Gilgamesh was also the hero of a famous ancient poem, the *Epic of Gilgamesh*.

About Gilgamesh

According to an ancient list of kings, Gilgamesh was the fifth king of the city of Uruk. The *Epic of Gilgamesh* tells the story of Gilgamesh and his friend, Enkidu, and the dangerous quests they went on together.

Find out more

Information about Gilgamesh can be found at: www.pantheon.org/articles/g/gilgamesh.html

Timeline

c. **2600 BC**	c. **2150–2000 BC**	c. **AD 1880**
Rule of Gilgamesh	Earliest Sumerian version of the *Epic of Gilgamesh* appears	First translation of the *Epic of Gilgamesh* into English

---

Sargon of Akkad

Sargon the Great was king of the Akkadians. He conquered **Sumer** in the 24th century BC. He went on to rule over the first great Mesopotamian **empire**.

About Sargon

In around 2400 BC, Sumer was overrun by the Akkadians, a people from a land to the north of Sumer. Sargon seized the throne of the Sumerian city of Kish. A brilliant soldier, he went on to attack Uruk. He later conquered the whole of Sumer.

Find out more

Look at a history website about Sargon and the Akkadian culture at: www.historyforkids.org/learn/westasia/history/akkadians.htm

Timeline

c. **2360 BC**	c. **2334 BC**	c. **2279 BC**	c. **2159 BC**
Sargon born	Seizes throne of Kish	Sargon dies	Collapse of Akkadian Empire

4

Hammurabi

A great king of Babylon, Hammurabi expanded the borders of his kingdom and became the most powerful ruler in the region. He is also remembered for creating a code of laws.

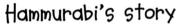

Hammurabi's story

In around 1792 BC, Hammurabi inherited the throne of Babylon, one of the many small city-states dotted across Mesopotamia. A skilled soldier and diplomat, Hammurabi led a series of wars against neighbouring cities and expanded his kingdom. Babylon became the region's leading city, and a great centre of culture and learning. By the time of Hammurabi's death, he controlled the whole of Mesopotamia from Babylon. In about 1595 BC, Babylon was overthrown by another group of people called the Hittites, who came from Anatolia (modern-day Turkey).

What he said

❝ Anum and Enlil named me to promote the welfare of the people, me, Hammurabi, the devout, god-fearing prince. ❞

Did you know?

Details of Hammurabi's life come from stone tablets created during his reign.

Timeline

Hammurabi born	Hammurabi dies	Stela of Code is discovered
c. 1810 BC c. 1792 BC c. 1750 BC c. 1595 BC AD 1901		

Becomes king of Babylon

Fall of Babylon

Find out more

A brief overview of Hammurabi's empire can be found at:
www.historyforkids.org/learn/westasia/history/hammurabi.htm

Read about Hammurabi's code and find links to further information at:
www.historyguide.org/ancient/hammurabi.html

Place in history

Apart from being a powerful ruler, Hammurabi was also concerned with law and order. He was responsible for the world's first written code of laws, known as "Hammurabi's Code". The Code was written on a stone slab, called a *stela*, and displayed in a public place so that everyone could see it. There were 282 laws in Hammurabi's Code, with each crime receiving a different punishment.

Tiglath-Pileser III

Tiglath-Pileser III was a warrior-king of **Assyria** in northern Mesopotamia in the 8th century BC. When he was king, the Assyrians ruled over a vast empire.

About Tiglath-Pileser III

Tiglath-Pileser seized the throne during a **civil war**. He went on to conquer Babylon, Syria, Armenia, and Phoenicia. These conquests helped to build a vast and powerful empire, called the New Assyrian Empire.

Find out more

See a photo of the tablet of Tiglath-Pileser III and read about its significance at: www.bible-history.com/archaeology/assyria/Tiglath-Pileser-III.html

Timeline

	Becomes king of Babylon	
c. **745 BC**	c. **729 BC**	c. **727 BC**
Seizes throne of Assyria		Dies and is succeeded by son, Shalmaneser V

Ashurbanipal II

The last great king of Assyria, Ashurbanipal ruled from around 669 to 627 BC. During his rule, Assyrian art and culture flourished.

About Ashurbanipal II

Ashurbanipal became king of Assyria when his father died suddenly in 669 BC. Ashurbanipal was a great warrior. Proud of his education, he also built a library at Nineveh where he collected texts from all over Mesopotamia.

Find out more

This site includes a short biography and a timeline of Ashurbanipal's life: www.lexicorient.com/e.o/ashurbanipal.htm

Timeline

Ashurbanipal II born		Ashurbanipal dies
c. **685 BC**	c. **669 BC**	c. **627 BC**
	Becomes king of Assyria	

Nebuchadnezzar II

King of Babylon from around 605 to 562, Nebuchadnezzar II rebuilt the city of Babylon and created the Hanging Gardens, one of the seven wonders of the ancient world.

Nebuchadnezzar's story

Nebuchadnezzar was the son of King Nabopolassar, who defeated the Assyrians and Babylon became powerful again. Nebuchadnezzar became king when his father died around 605 BC. Already an experienced soldier, he fought a series of military campaigns. He captured Syria and Palestine, and conquered the city of Jerusalem in 597 BC. In 587 BC, the King of Judah rebelled. Nebuchadnezzar **besieged** the city, which fell after 18 months. Then he destroyed the walls and temple and had many of the people carried off to Babylon.

What was said

❝ The approach to the Gardens sloped like a hillside… and was thickly planted with trees of every kind… ❞

Did you know?

Many events from Nebuchadnezzar's reign appear in the Book of Daniel in the Bible.

Timeline

Nebuchadnezzar born		Builds Hanging Gardens			Fall of Babylon
c. **630 BC**	c. **605 BC**	c. **600 BC**	c. **562 BC**	**539 BC**	
	Becomes king of Babylon		Dies in Babylon		

Find out more

Find out about the early years of Nebuchadnezzar II at: www.livius.org/cg-cm/chronicles/abc5/jerusalem.html

There is more information at the British Museum site: www.britishmuseum.org

Place in history

Under the Assyrians, the city of Babylon had been largely destroyed. Nebuchadnezzar rebuilt the city, making it more magnificent than ever before. He completed his father's fabulous palace and put up new temples to the gods. The city itself was protected by three lines of walls.

Nebuchadnezzar also built the Hanging Gardens of Babylon. According to legend, the gardens took the form of mountains, covered with trees and bushes. The king created the gardens for his wife, Amytis, who missed the trees and mountains of her homeland, **Medea**.

Menes

Menes, king of Upper Egypt, conquered Lower Egypt and united the two kingdoms in around 3100 BC. Menes was the first **pharaoh** of an united Egypt.

About Menes

Having united Upper and Lower Egypt, King Menes built a new capital at Memphis, on the border between the two regions. Tradition says that Menes reigned for more than 60 years. He was succeeded by his son, Hor-aha.

Find out more

Find out more information about Menes at:
www.mnsu.edu/emuseum/prehistory/egypt/history/people/menes.html

Timeline

Unifies Upper and Lower Egypt

c. **3107 BC**	c. **3100 BC**	c. **3046 BC**
Becomes king of Upper Egypt		Menes dies

Imhotep

Imhotep was an Egyptian priest, poet, and doctor in the 27th century BC. He was also the **architect** of the first pyramid, built for King Djoser at Saqqara.

About Imhotep

Imhotep served as chancellor and high priest for King Djoser. Imhotep is famous for designing the first pyramid as a tomb for the king. Built as a series of huge steps. It was originally covered in polished white limestone, and was surrounded by a courtyard.

Find out more

Read about the pyramid Imhotep built at:
www.touregypt.net/featurestories/dsteppyramid1.htm

Timeline

Djoser becomes pharaoh

Djoser dies

c. **2630 BC**	c. **2611 BC**

Imhotep designs first pyramid

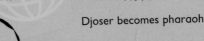

Khufu

King Khufu (also known as Cheops) was pharaoh of Egypt during the 26th century BC. His tomb, the Great Pyramid at Giza, is one of the seven wonders of the ancient world.

About Khufu

Khufu came to the throne around 2551 BC and reigned for about 23 years. During this time, he supervized the building of the Great Pyramid at Giza as his tomb. The largest of the Egyptian pyramids, it is the biggest stone structure ever built.

Find out more

Find out about the Great Pyramid at Giza on the "National Geographic" site: www.nationalgeographic.com/pyramids/khufu.html

Timeline

Khufu becomes pharaoh

c. **2551 BC**

c. **2528 BC**

Khufu dies

Pepi II

Pepi II reigned as Pharaoh of Egypt for 94 years in the 23rd and 22nd centuries BC. This is thought to be the longest reign in history.

About Pepi II

Pepi II came to the throne aged just six years old. During his long reign, the power of the nomarchs (regional governors) grew, and the pharaoh's power grew weaker. After his death, disputes broke out over who would succeed him. Egypt collapsed into chaos and confusion.

Find out more

Discover more about the life of Pepi II at: www.ancientegyptonline.co.uk/Pepill.html

Timeline

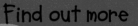

Pepi II born

Pepi II dies

c. **2252 BC**

c. **2246 BC**

c. **2152 BC**

Pepi II becomes pharaoh

Hatshepsut

One of the most remarkable rulers of ancient Egypt, Queen Hatshepsut was pharaoh from about 1490 to 1468 BC. She was originally appointed as regent for Tuthmosis III (⇨p11).

What she said

66 Hear ye, all persons… I have restored that which was in ruins… 99

How did she die?

Hatshepsut may have died of blood poisoning after having a tooth taken out.

Find out more

Lots of information about Hatshepsut can be found at:
www.bediz.com/hatshep

Read more about the discovery of her mummy at:
www.egyptologyonline.com/hatshepsut's_mummy.htm

Another great site is:
www.eyelid.co.uk/k-q1.htm

Hatshepsut's story

Hatshepsut was the daughter of Tuthmosis I and Queen Ahmose. She married Prince Tuthmosis, who became Tuthmosis II. When he died suddenly, her baby stepson became Tuthmosis III. The new pharaoh was too young to rule, and, at first, Hatshepsut was appointed as **regent**. Some time later, however, Hatshepsut had herself crowned "king" and became one of the very few female pharaohs in ancient Egyptian history.

Timeline

Hatshepsut is born

Hatshepsut dies

c. **1508 BC**   **1479 BC**   **1457 BC**

Becomes pharaoh

Place in history

Queen Hatshepsut's 20-year rule was peaceful and prosperous. She built magnificent temples and defended Egypt's borders from attack. She also sent a successful trading expedition to the land of Punt, possibly located on the east coast of Africa.

Hatshepsut built a magnificent funerary (burial) temple on the banks of the River Nile. The walls of the temple were decorated with paintings of the events in Hatshepsut's life, including the expedition to Punt. After her death, Tuthmosis III destroyed the temple's statues and inscriptions, perhaps because she had kept him out of power for so long.

Tuthmosis III

One of the greatest warrior-pharaohs of ancient Egypt, Tuthmosis III expanded the Egyptian empire until it reached its greatest ever size.

Tuthmosis's story

Tuthmosis III was the son of Tuthmosis II and his wife, Iset. His father died when Tuthmosis III was too young to rule. His stepmother, Hatshepsut (⇨p10), was appointed as an advisor but then declared herself pharaoh. For the next 20 years, Tuthmosis III did not have any real power. As a young man, he trained as a soldier and led the army on several wars. When Hatshepsut died he was at last able to rule in his own right.

What he said

❝ None shall go forth before my majesty. ❞

(Account of the Battle of Megiddo)

Find out more

Discover more about Tuthmosis III at:
www.mnsu.edu/emuseum/prehistory/egypt/history/people/tuthmosi_3.html

This site contains information about Tuthmosis's military campaigns.
www.egyptologyonline.com/tuthmosis_iii.htm

Timeline

Official reign begins

c. 1479 BC

c. 1457 BC

Hatshepsut dies; Tuthmosis III becomes pharaoh

Tuthmosis III dies

c. 1425 BC

Place in history

Tuthmosis III fought in 17 campaigns during his own reign. He conquered large parts of the Middle East, including Syria and Nubia (modern-day Sudan). He created the largest empire that Egypt had ever known. Details of his campaigns were written down by his royal **scribe**, Tjaneni. This record was later copied and engraved on the walls of the great Temple of Amun at Karnak.

During his reign, Tuthmosis III ordered the building of more than 50 temples and many tombs for nobles. When he died in around 1425 BC, he was buried in the Valley of the Kings in a tomb halfway up a cliff face. He was succeeded by his son, Amenhotep II.

Did you know?

Tuthmosis's **mummy** was found in the late 19th century and is now in the Cairo Museum.

Akhenaten

King Akhenaten ruled Egypt in the 14th century BC. During his reign, he shocked many Egyptians by making changes to their religion, including introducing the worship of only one god.

What was said

❝ Yabitiri, your servant, the dust of your feet, at the feet of my lord, my king, my gods, my sun, seven times and seven times more, I fall down. ❞

Did you know?

Found in 1887, the Amarna letters were sent to Akhenaten by rulers from all over the Middle East.

Akhenaten's story

First known as Amenhotep IV, Akhenaten was the son of Amenhotep III and Queen Tiye. He came to the throne because his elder brother, Tuthmose, died. Akhenaten was married to Queen Nefertiti (⇨p13) and had six daughters and possibly two sons. Later, Akhenaten appointed Smenkhare to help him rule Egypt. Smenkhare might have been his half-brother or son.

Timeline

Becomes pharaoh

Smenkhare helps rule Egypt

c. **1353 BC** c. **1343 BC** c. **1339 BC** c. **1336 BC**

Moves to Akhetaten

Akhenaten dies

Find out more

Find out about Ankhenaten's life at:
www.egyptologyonline.com/akhenaten1.htm

Learn about the Armana period on the BBC's site:
www.bbc.co.uk/history/ancient/egyptians/akhenaten_01.shtml

This site provides an account of his new religion:
http://famouspharaohs.blogspot.com/2007/10/ankhenaten-13501349-1334-b.html

Place in history

Before Akhenaten, the ancient Egyptians worshipped many different gods and goddesses. But Akhenaten introduced the worship of only one god, Aten, the sun god. In Aten's honour, he changed his name from Amenhotep to Akhenaten, which means "living spirit of the Aten". Legend says that he decided that Aten should have a city of his own, so he also built a new capital city, called Akhetaten.

Many ancient Egyptians were dismayed by the king's changes to their religion. After Akhenaten's death, the worship of many different gods was re-introduced. Akhetaten was abandoned, and the temples built by Akhenaten were destroyed.

Nefertiti

One of the most famous women of the ancient world, Nefertiti was the wife of King Akhenaten (⇨p12) and the Queen of Egypt.

Nefertiti's story

Little is known about Nefertiti's family, although some experts think that she may have been the daughter of Ay, who later became pharaoh. She married Akhenaten, and they had six daughters. Famous throughout the ancient world for her beauty, she was also very powerful. Apart from helping the king make his religious changes, she may also have been his co-ruler for a while in their new capital, Akhetaten. He gave her a second, official, name. Usually, only kings took a second name.

What was said

66 May she live for Ever and Always. 99

Akhenaten

Did you know?

In the 1900s, Nefertiti's sculptured head was found in ruins in Tell el Amarna.

Timeline

Nefertiti born		Akhenaten dies	
c. **1370 BC**	c. **1339 BC**	c. **1336 BC**	c. **1330 BC**
	Nefertiti dies?		Nefertiti dies?

Place in history

It is not certain if Nefertiti died before or after her husband. One theory is that she became pharaoh in her own right on Akhenaten's death and ruled for a few years. She was succeeded by her son-in-law, Tutankhamun (⇨p14), who married her daughter, Ankhesenamun. Her tomb and mummy have not yet been discovered.

Find out more

Read about Nefertiti at:
www.akhet.co.uk/nefertit.htm

This site has lots of information about Nefertiti, including lots of pictures:
www.crystalinks.com/nefertiti.html

Another great site is:
www.touregypt.net/featurestories/nefertiti.htm

Tutankhamun

Although King Tutankhamun died very young, he is one of the most famous of the Egyptian pharaohs because of the priceless treasures found in his tomb in the 1920s.

What was said

66 All we have to do is peel the shrines like an onion, and we will be with the king himself. 99

Did you know?

Some experts think that Tutankhamun died of gangrene after breaking his leg.

Tutankhamun's story

Tutankhamun was the son of Akhenaten (⇨p12). He became pharaoh at the age of eight or nine and ruled for about ten years. He married his half-sister, Ankhesenamun, the daughter of Queen Nefertiti (⇨p13). An official, called Ay, and a general, called Horemheb, helped the young king rule. They moved the capital city from Akhetaten back to Thebes. They also brought back the worship of all the Egyptians gods. Tutankhamun died at the age of 18 or 19. He was succeeded first by Ay, and then by Horemheb.

Timeline

Tutankhamun born

Tutankhamun dies

c. **1341 BC**   c. **1333 BC**   c. **1323 BC**   **AD 1922**

Becomes pharaoh

Carter discovers tomb

Find out more

This site has lots of information and images:
www.civilization.ca/civil/egypt/egtut01e.html

This site Includes a photo gallery, online tour, and interactive exploration of his tomb:
www.fieldmuseum.org/tut

This site is all about ancient Egypt:
www.eternalegypt.org

Place in history

In 1922, British **archaeologist**, Howard Carter, made an astonishing discovery. He unearthed the tomb of Tutankhamun in the Valley of the Kings in Egypt. Most of the royal tombs had been plundered by tomb-robbers, but Tutankhamun's had survived almost intact. Until then, little had been known about Tutankhamun, but this discovery turned him into a star. Among the extraordinary treasures Carter found was a set of three golden coffins. In the inner coffin lay Tutankhamun's mummy, covered by a solid gold death mask.

Cleopatra VII

Cleopatra VII was Queen of Egypt from 51 to 30 BC. She is still famous today for her relationships with the Romans, Julius Caesar (⇨p27) and Mark Antony.

Cleopatra's story

Cleopatra was the daughter of Ptolemy XII and Cleopatra V. When her father died in 51 BC, she ruled Egypt with her brother, Ptolemy XIII. A clever politician, she brought peace to war-torn Egypt. In 48 BC, Egypt became involved in the civil war that was going on in Rome. Julius Caesar seized the Egyptian capital. Cleopatra was thrown out of Egypt by her brother. She returned and became Caesar's lover. With his support, she won back her throne.

What she said

" All strange and terrible events are welcome, but comforts we despise. "

Timeline

Cleopatra born		Marries Mark Anthony		Cleopatra dies	
69 BC	51 BC	37 BC	31 BC	30 BC	
	Becomes Queen of Egypt		Battle of Actium		

Find out more

Learn about Cleopatra:
www.bbc.co.uk/history/historic_figures/cleopatra_vii.shtml

Read more about Cleopatra at:
www.touregypt.net/cleopatr.htm

Another useful site is:
www.mymacedonia.net/cleopatra/cleopatra.htm

A few years after Caesar was murdered, Cleopatra married the Roman general, Mark Antony. Antony was in conflict with Caesar's son, Octavian. In 31 BC, Cleopatra and Mark Antony joined forces against Octavian but were defeated at the Battle of Actium. Cleopatra and Mark Antony both committed suicide.

Place in history

Cleopatra was the last of the Ptolemaic rulers of Egypt. They were descended from Ptolemy, one of the generals of Alexander the Great (⇨p25). In 332 BC, Alexander made Egypt part of his empire. Ptolemy declared himself pharaoh in 305 BC, and began the Ptolemaic **Dynasty**.

How did she die?

It is said that Cleopatra committed suicide by getting a poisonous snake to bite her.

Homer

Homer was an ancient Greek poet who composed two poems, called *The Iliad* and *The Odyssey*. These are two of the most important works of Greek literature.

What he said

❝ Once harm has been done, even a fool understands it. **❞**

(The Iliad)

Did you know?

In 1870, Heinrich Schliemann dug up a city in Turkey that he later identified as Troy.

Find out more

Read about "The Iliad" and "The Odyssey":
http://library.thinkquest.org/19300/data/homer.htm

Look at the BBC site about Homer:
www.bbc.co.uk/history/historic_figures/homer.shtml

Read more about Homer's life at:
www.wsu.edu/~dee/MINOA/HOMER.HTM

Homer's story

Very little is known about Homer's life. According to tradition, he came from the Greek island of Chiops, and he may have been blind. In carvings and sculptures, he is usually shown with a beard. Homer was a bard, or storyteller. He told his stories, in poem form, to gatherings of people, taking several days to complete each tale. The poems were not written down until centuries after his death.

Timeline

Life of Homer; Homer composes *The Iliad* and *The Odyssey*

City of Troy built

c. 3600 BC   **c. 1250 BC**   **c. 750–650 BC**   **AD 1870**

Possible date of Trojan War

Schliemann excavates Troy

Place in history

Both *The Iliad* and *The Odyssey* tell the story of events around the Trojan War. They are thought to have been written between about 750–650 BC. *The Iliad* is the story of the Greek hero, Achilles, who is famous for his strength and bravery, and kills the Trojan hero, Hector. *The Odyssey* tells of another Greek hero, Odysseus. It was his idea to send a wooden horse filled with soldiers into Troy. This trick won the war for the Greeks. Afterwards, Odysseus was given the choice of becoming **immortal** like the gods or returning home as a **mortal** human. He chose to return home to Greece.

Sappho

Although very little of her work survives, Sappho is regarded as one of the greatest ancient Greek poets, and the most important female poet of ancient times.

Sappho's story

Very little is known about Sappho's life. Different ancient writers give different accounts. It seems that Sappho was born between 630 and 612 BC on the Greek island of Lesbos. She is reported to have had three brothers and may have come from an noble and wealthy family. In one of her poems, she mentions a girl called Cleis, who may have been her daughter. At some point, Sappho left Lesbos and either travelled to, or was **exiled** to, Sicily, an island off Italy. She later returned home, and spent the rest of her life there, dying in around 570 BC.

What she said

66 If you are my friend, stand up before me and scatter the grace that is in your eyes. 99

Did you Know?

One of Sappho's poems was found on the papyrus used to wrap an Egyptian mummy.

Timeline

Sappho born

c. **630–612 BC**

c. **604–594 BC**

Possibly exiled to Sicily

Sappho dies

c. **570 BC**

Find out more

This site includes some of Sappho's poetry:
http://oldpoetry.com/oauthor/show/Sappho

Find out more about Sappho at:
http://womenshistory.about.com/library/bio/blbio_sappho.htm

Place in history

Tradition says that Sappho wrote nine books of love poetry, but only fragments of her work have survived. In Sappho's own lifetime, her poetry was very well known and much admired. Indeed, Sappho's poetry is featured in the work of many other ancient writers. Today, Sappho's work is still widely read and studied and has inspired other many other writers and poets.

Pythagoras

Pythagoras was an ancient Greek **philosopher** and mathematician. He is famous for his theorem (rule) on triangles, which is named after him.

What he said

66 Number is the ruler of forms and ideas, and the cause of gods and demons. 99

Did you know?

Pythagoras believed that the Earth was round, and that the planets orbited the Sun.

Find out more

A BBC site about Pythagoras and his followers is:
www.bbc.co.uk/history/historic_figures/pythagoras.shtml

Read about the life of Pythagoras at:
http://library.thinkquest.org/4116/History/pythagor.htm

This is another useful site:
www.historyforkids.org/learn/greeks

Pythagoras's story

Pythagoras was born on the Greek island of Samos in about 581 BC. His father was a merchant from Phoenicia (modern-day Lebanon). As a young man, Pythagoras may have travelled to Egypt. He later moved to Croton in southern Italy, where he set up a philosophical school. His followers, called Pythagoreans, lived a strict life of teaching, exercise, and study. Among other things, they studied the relationship between mathematics and the world around them. Towards the end of his life, Pythagoras was forced to flee to the city of Metapontum because of a plot against him and his followers.

Timeline

Born in Samos

Moves to Metapontum

c. **581 BC**   c. **518 BC**   c. **500 BC**   c. **497 BC**

Establishes a school at Croton

Dies in Metapontum

Place in history

Together with other ancient Greek scholars, Pythagoras worked out many of the basic rules of mathematics. These rules are still used today. Pythagoras is best remembered for Pythagoras's Theorem. It states that, in a right-angled triangle, the square of the hypotenuse (the longest side) equals the sum of the squares of the other two sides. This means that once you know the lengths of two sides of any right-angled triangle, you can work out the length of the third side.

Pericles

The most popular politician of his day, Pericles came from a powerful family and was a leading statesman and general of Athens during the city's Golden Age.

Pericles's story

Pericles was born in Athens, Greece, in around 495 BC into a noble family. His father was a powerful politician. As a boy, Pericles enjoyed his studies, learning music and philosophy. Gradually, he became involved in the city's politics. In 443 BC, Pericles was elected strategos for the first time. A strategos was a military commander, responsible for putting new laws into action. Pericles proved so popular that he was elected to office every year until his death in 429 BC. Famous for his calmness, he was such a powerful speaker that he was almost always able to win the public over to his way of thinking.

What he said

❝ But the bravest are surely those who have the clearest vision of what is before them… ❞

Find out more

This site gives an account of Pericles's life:
www.usefultrivia.com/biographies/pericles_001.html

Find out more about Pericles at:
www.pbs.org/empires/thegreeks/htmlver/characters/f_pericles.html

Timeline

Born in Athens, Greece	First elected as strategos		Dies in Athens
c. 495 BC	479–431 BC	443 BC	431 BC	429 BC
	Golden Age of Athens	Start of Peloponnesian War	

Place in history

Pericles had such a great influence on Athens that the ancient Greek historian, Thucydides called him "the first citizen of Athens". Under his leadership, the city enjoyed good times. Science, philosophy, and the arts flourished. In politics, he helped to refine the **democratic** system of government in Athens, making life better for the poor. A brilliant soldier, he also led the Athenians during the first two years of the Peloponnesian War between Athens and another city-state, Sparta.

How did he die?

Pericles died of plague that swept across Athens, killing one-quarter of the population.

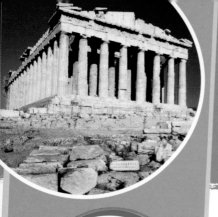

Phidias

Phidias was an extremely talented sculptor and painter and the most famous artist of the ancient world. He designed the marble carving that runs around the Parthenon (top left).

Did you know?

In 1958, the ruins of Phidias's workshop at Olympia were found.

Phidias's life

Very little is known about the life of Phidias. It is said that he was born in Athens and learned about art by talking to other famous Greek sculptors. He may have worked as a painter before becoming a sculptor. In the mid-5th century BC, his friend Pericles (⇨p19) began rebuilding the city of Athens. He asked Phidias to help with this work. When Pericles fell out of favour, Phidias also suffered. He was accused of stealing some of the gold given to him for the statue of Athena he was making. He supposedly cleared his name, only to be thrown into prison on another charge.

Find out more

This site has links to images of Phidias's works:
www.artcyclopedia.com/artists/phidias.html

More information about Phidias can be found at:
www.ancientgreece.com/s/People/Phidias

The British Museum website is:
www.britishmuseum.org

Timeline

Born in Athens
c. 500 BC

Commissioned by Pericles
c. 447 BC

Dies in Athens
c. 425 BC

How did he die?

It is thought that Phidias died in prison in Athens.

Place in history

In ancient times, Phidias was famous for two works in particular, although neither has survived. One was a huge, seated statue of the god, Zeus, at Olympia. The other is a colossal statue of the goddess, Athena, which stood inside the Parthenon. Phidias also designed the amazing carved marble frieze around the Parthenon. You could visit the British Museum in London to see it.

Herodotus

Herodotus was an ancient Greek historian who wrote one of the first known history books. He also travelled widely and wrote about the places that he visited.

Herodotus's story

It is believed that Herodotus was born in about 484 BC in Halicarnassus. This was a city in south-west Asia Minor (modern-day Turkey), which was then under Persian rule. Later, he may have spent some time in Athens, before settling in Thurii in southern Italy. Herodotus seems to have travelled widely in the Middle East and North Africa. On his travels, he collected huge amounts of information on the history, geography, and culture of the places he visited. It is not known where or how he died.

What he said

66 Circumstances rule men; men do not rule circumstances. 99

Did you know?

Herodotus's report on Egypt includes a detailed account of mummification.

Timeline

Start of Persian Wars		End of Persian Wars			Dies in Thurii or Pella
490 BC	c. 484 BC	c. 479 BC	c. 431–425 BC	c. 420 BC	
	Born in Halicarnassus		Writes *The Histories*		

Find out more

Read a short biography of Herodotus:
www.historyguide.org/ancient/herodotus.html

An account of his life and the times in which he lived:
www.livius.org/he-hg/herodotus/herodotus01.htm

Herodotus's "The Histories" can be found at:
http://classics.mit.edu/Herodotus/history.html

Place in history

Herodotus is best known for his book, *The Histories*, which is one of the first history books. The book describes the story of the Persian Wars fought between Persia and Greece. Herodotus based his account on interviews with survivors of the wars and their families. He also describes the Persian Empire and its rulers. *The Histories* is also a travel book, describing the people and places he visited. Some of his accounts are not strictly accurate but he said that he only reported what he had been told.

Socrates

Socrates was an ancient Greek philosopher who lived in Athens in the 5th century BC. He was one of the most important philosophers in history.

What he said

66 The only good is knowledge and the only evil is ignorance. 99

How did he die?

Socrates was forced to kill himself by drinking a cup of poison.

Socrates's story

Socrates did not write anything down so what we know of his life comes mainly what his students have written about him, especially the philosopher, Plato. Socrates was born in around 469 BC. After his education, Socrates got married and served in the Greek army. When he left the army, he turned to philosophy. He taught by word of mouth, in public places like the market place. Socrates criticized the government of Athens, and this made him unpopular with the city's leaders.

Timeline

c. **469 BC**	c. **428 BC**	**399 BC**	c. **348 BC**
Born in Athens	Plato born in Athens	Trial of Socrates; Socrates dies	Plato dies

Find out more

Read about Socrates's life at:
www.historyforkids.org/learn/greeks/philosophy/socrates.htm

Read some quotes by Socrates at:
www.quotationspage.com/quotes/Socrates

Find out more about Socrates at:
www.philosophypages.com/ph/socr.htm

In 399 BC, at the age of 70, he was put on trial and charged with disobeying religious laws. He was sentenced to death.

Place in history

Socrates's ideas formed the basis of the study of philosophy and are still widely studied today. Socrates believed that people would behave well if they knew what good behaviour was. His way of teaching was to encourage his students to make their own minds up. He challenged them to think about truth, good and evil, by asking them questions to help them form their own beliefs.

Hippocrates

Hippocrates was a famous Greek doctor whose teachings revolutionized medical practice throughout the ancient world.

Hippocrates's story

Born in around 460 BC on the Greek island of Kos, Hippocrates became a doctor and teacher of medicine. He may have trained at the temple of Asclepius, the Greek god of healing. Hippocrates spent most of his life on Kos where he founded an important medical school. Unlike other doctors of the time, he taught his students to look for the scientific causes of illnesses rather than relying on religious rituals. This approach revolutionized ancient medicine. Many of his students went on to open schools where this new type of medicine was taught.

What he said

66 I will prescribe regimens for the good of my patients according to my ability and my judgment and never do harm to anyone. 99

Find out more

Find out about Hippocrates's influence on the history of medicine at: www.historylearningsite.co.uk/hippocrates.htm

This site explains the Hippocratic oath: www.bbc.co.uk/dna/h2g2/A1103798

Another good site is: www.schoolshistory.org.uk/hippocrates.htm

Timeline

Dies in Kos

c. **460 BC**   c. **377 BC**

Born in Kos

Place in history

Hippocrates and his students were the first to describe many medical conditions, some of which are named after him. He is also remembered in modern medicine for the Hippocratic Oath. This was an oath (promise) that he expected his students to swear to ensure good medical practice. In Hippocratic Oath, his students promised to use medicine to heal, not harm, not to give poison, and not to betray a patient's confidence. A similar oath is still taken today by newly qualified doctors.

Did you know?

The snake was linked with Asclepius in ancient Greek. It is still used as a symbol of medicine.

Aristotle

One of the greatest philosophers of ancient Greece, Aristotle also worked as the tutor to Alexander the Great (⇨p25).

What he said

66 He who has overcome his fears will truly be free. 99

Did you know?

Aristotle's followers were called the "peripatetics", which means "those who walk about".

Aristotle's story

Aristotle was born in Stagiros, Macedonia, where his father was the royal doctor. When his father died, Aristotle was sent to Athens, Greece. He studied at the Academy, the school set up by the philosopher, Plato, and later became a teacher there. Later, he returned to Macedonia where he became tutor to Alexander the Great. In 335 BC, Aristotle went back to Athens and set up his own school, called the Lyceum. After Alexander's death, Aristotle left Athens. He went to live on the island of Euboea, where he later died.

Timeline

Born in Stagiros, Macedon

Tutor to Alexander the Great

Alexander the Great dies

384 BC c. **367 BC** c. **343–335 BC** **335 BC** **323 BC** **322 BC**

Enters the Academy in Athens

Returns to Athens and sets up the Lyceum

Dies in Euboea

Find out more

Find out more about Aristotle at:
www.philosophypages.com/ph/aris.htm

Read some quotes by Aristotle at:
www.quotationspage.com/quotes/Aristotle/

Another great site is:
www.historyforkids.org/learn/greeks/philosophy/aristotle.htm

Place in history

Aristotle's work covers many different subjects, from poetry and philosophy to science and natural history. Aristotle's ideas had a great influence on Western thinking for almost 2,000 years after his death and are still studied today.

Alexander the Great

King of Macedonia, and a brilliant military leader, Alexander the Great conquered the largest empire in the ancient world. It stretched from Macedonia in the west as far as India in the east.

Alexander's story

Born in the northern Greek kingdom of Macedonia, Alexander was the son of King Philip II and Queen Olympias. He was educated by the philosopher, Aristotle (⇨p24). In 336 BC, Philip was killed, and Alexander came to the throne at the age of just 20. First, Alexander defeated his enemies in Macedonia. He then set out to conquer the mighty Persian Empire.

What he said

❝ I am not afraid of an army of lions led by a sheep. I am afraid of an army of sheep led by a lion. ❞

How did he die?

Alexander died at the age of 32, possibly of typhoid fever.

Timeline

Born in Pella, Macedonia	Battle of Gaugamela		Dies in Babylon
356 BC	**336 BC**	**331 BC**	**326 BC**	**323 BC**
	Becomes King of Macedonia		Reaches India

Place in history

Over the next 13 years, Alexander changed the face of the ancient world. A military genius, he conquered an empire one-third larger than the Roman Empire. Having defeated the Persians, he led his army a further 17,000 kilometres (10,500 miles). He set up more than 70 cities and an empire that covered three continents. By 326 BC, Alexander had reached north-west India.

Alexander left Greek governors behind in all the places he conquered. This helped to unite the different parts of his empire and to spread Greek language and culture across a huge area. Long after Alexander's death, Greek style and ideas continued to influence these places.

Find out more

Read about Alexander the Great: www.bbc.co.uk/history/historic_figures/alexander_the_great.shtml

Find out more about the history of Macedonia at: www.historyofmacedonia.org

Further information about Alexander the Great can be found at: www.wsu.edu/~dee/GREECE/ALEX.HTM

Cicero

The greatest public speaker of his day, Cicero was a Roman politician and writer. He became a famous lawyer and was elected as consul of Rome.

What he said

66 Though silence is not necessarily an admission, it is not a denial, either. 99

How did he die?

Cicero was beheaded in 43 BC, and his head was displayed in the Roman Forum.

Cicero's story

Marcus Tullius Cicero was born in Arpinium in 106 BC. A brilliant student, he excelled in Latin, Greek, Roman law, and philosophy. Cicero began his career as a lawyer in about 83 BC. Later, he went to Athens to study public speaking. Back in Rome, his speeches in the law courts made him famous. In 63 BC, Cicero was elected consul (a representative of Rome), but he made many enemies. After Caesar's death in 44 BC, he spoke out against Mark Antony, who wanted to follow Caesar as ruler of Rome. Antony later had Cicero **assassinated**.

Timeline

Born in Arpinium, Italy		Enters politics		Julius Caesar dies	
106 BC	c. 83 BC	c. 75 BC	63 BC	44 BC	43 BC
	Begins career in law		Elected consul		Dies in Formia, Italy

Find out more

This site is full of information, images, and links:
www.iep.utm.edu/c/cicero.htm

Discover more about Cicero at:
www.utexas.edu/depts/classics/documents/Cic.html

Read some quotes by Cicero at:
www.quotationspage.com/quotes/Cicero

Place in history

Cicero's style of speaking and writing were so highly thought of that they were copied for centuries after his death. Many of his speeches, letters, and writings on politics and philosophy have survived. They tell us a great deal about what life was like in Rome. They also show that Cicero was responsible for introducing many Greek ideas to the Romans.

Julius Caesar

Julius Caesar was a brilliant soldier and politician who greatly extended Roman territory. He went on to seize power and made himself **dictator**.

Caesar's story

Caesar was born into a powerful Roman family. He joined the army and was a fine soldier. Later, he turned to politics. In 60 BC, Caesar was elected as consul. The following year, he was made governor of Gaul (modern-day France), where he stayed for eight years. During this time, he invaded and conquered most of Britain.

What he said

66 Veni, vidi, vici. 99

("I came, I saw, I conquered".)

Timeline

Born in Rome on 12 or 13 July	Leads a series of campaigns in Gaul		Dies in Rome
c. 100 or 102 BC c. 59 BC	c. 58-49 BC	c. 55-54 BC	44 BC
Elected as consul of Rome	Leads the invasion of Britain		

Find out more

Lots of information about Caesar can be found at:
http://rome.mrdonn.org/

Find out more about Caesar at:
www.eyewitnesstohistory.com/caesar2.htm

Caesar returned to Italy in 49 BC. Soon after, a civil war broke out. Caesar defeated Pompey, Rome's ruler. He became the most powerful man in Rome. He used his power to pass laws to help the poor and improve the administration. Caesar was declared ruler for life.

Place in history

Much about Caesar's life is known from his own writings. These works include his notes on the Gallic Wars, in which he describes the years he spent fighting in Gaul. Caesar dictated his words to a scribe. Caesar was murdered by a group of **senators**. His death marked the end of the Roman **Republic** and the beginning of the Roman Empire.

How did he die?

Caesar was murdered on 15 March 44 BC by a group of senators.

Virgil

Virgil was a great Roman poet. He wrote the **epic** poem, *Aeneid*, which tells the story of Aeneas, a hero of the Trojan War.

What he said

66 If I cannot bend Heaven, I shall move Hell. 99

How did he die?

Virgil died of a fever at the age of 51.

Find out more

Learn about Virgil:
www.bbc.co.uk/history/historic_figures/virgil.shtml

This site has lots of information about Virgil:
www.users.globalnet.co.uk/~loxias/latin.htm

Read more about Virgil and his writing at:
www.kirjasto.sci.fi/virgil.htm

Virgil's story

Virgil was born in Mantua in northern Italy, where he spent his early life. In around 42 BC, his land was taken by the government and used to pay off retired soldiers. Later, Virgil met the wealthy Roman statesman, Gaius Maecenas, who gave him financial support. This allowed Virgil to dedicate himself to writing full time. During the last ten years of his life, Virgil worked on *Aeneid*, his most famous poem. On his deathbed, he is said to have wanted *Aeneid* burned. Emperor Augustus ignored his wishes and ordered it to be published.

Timeline

Born in Mantua, Italy		Publishes the *Georgics*		Dies in Brundisium, Italy
70 BC	mid-30s BC	29 BC	27 BC	19 BC
	Publishes the *Eclogues*		Octavian becomes Emperor Augustus	

Place in history

Today, Virgil is still remembered for his three great works: the *Eclogues*, the *Georgics*, and the *Aeneid*. The *Eclogues* is a series of poems about country life. The *Georgics* is about farming and politics. The *Aeneid* is an epic poem, divided into twelve books. The *Aeneid* tells the story of the Trojan hero, Aeneas. After the Trojan War, Aeneas travels to Italy. His descendants founded the city of Rome.

Augustus

Previously known as Octavian, Augustus was the first **emperor** of Rome. His long reign was a time of peace and stability for Rome after years of unrest.

Augustus's story

Augustus was born in Rome in 63 BC. Known as Octavian, he was the nephew and adopted son of Julius Caesar (⇨p27). When Caesar was murdered, Octavian joined forces with Mark Antony and his ally, Lepidus, to take over Rome. Later, Octavian and Antony split Roman territory between them. Octavian went on to defeat Antony and Cleopatra (⇨p15) at the Battle of Actium. He was given the new name "Augustus" ("revered one") and became the first Roman emperor.

What he said

66 I found Rome [made] of clay. I leave it to you [made] of marble. 99

Did you know?

Declared a god after his death, the month August was named in Augustus's honour.

Timeline

Born in Rome, Italy		Battle of Actium		Augustus dies at Nola, Italy
63 BC	**44 BC**	**31 BC**	**27 BC**	**AD 14**
	Julius Caesar dies		Becomes Rome's first emperor	

Place in history

Augustus set about rebuilding the city and securing Rome's borders from attack. By ruling cleverly and firmly, Augustus brought peace back to Rome.

Augustus had no sons and wanted his nephew or one of his grandsons to succeed him, but they died when they were young. Eventually, he named his stepson, Tiberius, as his heir. Augustus did not like Tiberius, but the two men ruled side by side for the last ten years of Augustus's life.

Find out more

Find out more about Augustus at: www.roman-emperors.org/ auggie.htm

This site has a timeline of events in his life: www.livius.org/au-az/augustus/ augustus.html

Another great site: www.vroma.org/~bmcmanus/ augustus.html

Livy

Livy was a famous Roman historian who wrote a great history of Rome and its people. Livy's writing filled 142 books but only 35 survive.

What he said

66 All things will be clear to the person who does not hurry. Haste is blind and improvident. 99

Did you know?

Roman schoolchildren may have used *Ab Urbe Condita* as a textbook.

Find out more

Find out more about Livy at:
www.livius.org/li-ln/livy/livy.htm

Read about Livy's life at:
http://academic.reed.edu/humanities/110Tech/Livy.html

This site includes an account of Livy's history of Rome:
http://etext.virginia.edu/toc/modeng/public/Liv1His.html

Livy's story

Livy was born in Padua, Italy, in about 59 BC. Nothing is known about his family, although it seems that Livy was well educated. Livy lived in interesting times, which he later recorded in his work. He witnessed a series of civil wars in Rome, after which Augustus became emperor. He wrote most of *Ab Urbe Condita* ("From the Founding of the City") during Augustus's rule (➪p29). Livy's writing brought him instant fame and wealth.

Timeline

Born in Padua, Italy

Augustus becomes emperor

| c. **59 BC** | c. **29 BC** | **27 BC** | c. **AD 17** |

Begins to write *Ab Urbe Condita*

Dies in Padua, Italy

Place in history

Ab Urbe Condita is a huge history of Rome and its people, from the founding of the city in 753 BC to the reign of Augustus and Livy's own time. The work was published in installments (parts) in sets of ten. Most of Livy's original work has been lost. Fragments continue to be found, most recently in Egypt.

Livia

Livia was the wife of the Emperor Augustus (➡p29). She was also the mother of Augustus's successor, Tiberius.

About Livia

Livia was born in 58 BC into one of the oldest Roman families. She divorced her first husband to marry Augustus and became the most powerful woman in the early Roman Empire. Tradition says that she was very wise.

Find out more

Find out more about Livia at:
www.livius.org/li-ln/
livia/livia.html

Read about Livia's life at:
www.roman-emperors.org/livia.htm

Timeline

Born in Rome, Italy		Augustus dies		Declared a god
58 BC	39 BC	AD 14	AD 29	AD 42
	Marries Augustus		Livia dies	

Agrippina

Agrippina was the mother of the Roman emperor, Nero (➡p32). She married another emperor, Claudius, whom she is said to have poisoned.

About Agrippina

Agrippina was involved in a plot to kill the emperor Caligula and was **banished** from Rome. Her uncle, Claudius, allowed her to return and married her. It is said that she later poisoned Claudius so that Nero could become emperor.

Find out more

Find out about Agrippina at:
www.roman-emperors.org/
aggieii.htm

More stories about Agrippina can be found at:
www.ancientsites.com/aw/
Thread/116676

Timeline

Born in Germany		Banished from Rome		Claudius dies	
AD 15	AD 37	AD 39	AD 49	AD 54	AD 59
	Nero born		Marries Claudius		Agrippina dies

Nero

Nero was the fifth Roman emperor who came to power in AD 54. He is remembered as being a cruel, arrogant, and weak ruler who was eventually forced out of Rome.

What he said

❝ What an artist dies in me! ❞

How did he die?

Nero committed suicide after being declared a public enemy of Rome.

Nero's story

Nero was born near Rome in AD 37 and was known as Domitius as a child. His mother was Agrippina (⇨p31). In AD 39 Agrippina married Emperor Claudius. She wanted Domitius to become the next emperor. So she had Claudius's own son, Britannicus, poisoned. Claudius adopted Domitius, who became known as Nero.

Timeline

Born near Rome, Italy		Murders mother		Nero dies
AD 37	**AD 54**	**AD 59**	**AD 64**	**AD 68**
	Becomes emperor		Fire destroys Rome	

Find out more

Discover more about Nero's life at:
www.roman-emperors.org/nero.htm

Thi site has more about Nero:
www.bbc.co.uk/history/historic_figures/
nero.shtml

Claudius died in AD 54, and Nero became emperor. Nero ruled sensibly at first, thanks to the guidance of his advisors, but he soon became power crazy. He had his enemies, including his mother, murdered. He increased taxes to pay for public shows that he put on in Rome. Meanwhile, costly wars and revolts plunged the Roman Empire into turmoil.

Place in history

Nero is best remembered for the fire that destroyed large parts of Rome in AD 64. It was rumoured that Nero himself started it, but he accused the Christians and began to kill them. He also started to rebuild the city, including a large, new villa for himself, known as the "Golden House". In AD 68, the Roman army rose up against Nero and forced him out of Rome.

Hadrian

Hadrian was emperor of Rome from AD 117–138. A great soldier, he spent more than half of his rule touring the Roman **provinces** with the army.

Hadrian's story

Hadrian joined the army as a young man. When his parents died, he was looked after by Emperor Trajan and named as his successor. He became emperor in AD 117. Hadrian spent much of his reign away from Rome, visiting the provinces and protecting the borders of the empire from attack. He also studied philosophy and gave lots of money to the arts. He built a beautiful villa at Tivoli outside Rome and a library in Athens, Greece.

What he said

" Little soul, wandering and pale, guest and companion of my body, you who will now go off to barren places... "

Did you know?

Hadrian's Wall was 4.5 metres (15 feet) high and 3 metres (10 feet) thick in places.

Timeline

Born in Rome, Italy	First tour to Germany		Dies in Baiae, Italy	
AD 76	**AD 117**	**AD 121**	**AD 122–129**	**AD 138**
	Becomes emperor		Builds Hadrian's Wall in Britain	

Find out more

Read the story of Hadrian's life at: www.roman-emperors.org/hadrian.htm

A site dedicated to Hadrian's wall, with lots of images: www.hadrians-wall.org

Discover more about Hadrian at: http://museums.ncl.ac.uk/WALLNET

Place in history

Hadrian is particularly famous for the strong walls he built to protect the Roman empire. Hadrian's Wall in Britain is the best preserved example. It was built between AD 122 and 129. The wall runs for almost 130 kilometres (81 miles) across northern Britain, from the River Tyne to the River Solway. It was built by the soldiers of the Roman army in Britain. Sixteen large forts were built into the wall, housing up to 1,000 soldiers.

Hadrian returned to Rome to spend the final years of his life there. He died in AD 138 at the age of 62. He was succeeded by Antoninus Pius.

Constantine

The first Christian emperor of Rome, Constantine moved the capital city from Rome to the new city of Constantinople (modern-day Istanbul in Turkey)

What he said

66 With this sign, you will conquer. 99

(On seeing a cross in the sky)

How did he die?

Constantine died in AD 337 at the age of 63. He formally became a Christian on his deathbed.

Find out more

Find out more about Constantine at: www.earlychurch.org.uk/constantine.php

Another good site: www.historyworld.net/wrldhis/PlainTextHistories.asp?historyid=ac60

A detailed page about Constantine can be found at: www.roman-emperors.org/conniei.htm

Constantine's story

At the time of Constantine, the Roman Empire was split into east and west – each with an emperor. Constantius, Constantine's father, was emperor of the the west. Diocletian was emperor of the east. When his father died, Constantine returned to Rome and defeated Diocletian, for overall power. He then set about reuniting the empire and became sole ruler in AD 323.

Timeline

Born in Naissus, Serbia

Constantinople becomes new capital

AD 274   AD 323   AD 330   AD 337

Becomes sole emperor

Dies in Constantinople

Constantine decided to move the capital of his new empire away from Rome. He rebuilt the city of Byzantium on the Black Sea (in modern-day Turkey) and renamed it Constantinople. It grew into a great and powerful city, and remained an important city for more than 1,000 years after Constantine's death.

Place in history

Constantine is most famous for being the first Christian Roman emperor. Under Diocletian, Christians had been badly treated. In AD 313, however, Constantine issued the Edict of Milan. The Edict allowed Christians to worship freely. This was a turning point for the Christian Church.

Confucius

Also known as K'ung Fu-tzu, Confucius was a religious teacher and philosopher whose ideas and teachings are still very important in China and East Asia today.

Confucius's story

Confucius was born in the state of Lu, near modern-day Shantung, China. It is thought that he came from a noble family who had fallen on hard times. He spent his early life working as a civil servant in the government. However, he was also interested in finding the best way to behave and live in the world. At the age of about 50, he gave up his job and began travelling the country and spreading his ideas. He quickly gained many followers. After his death in around 479 BC, his grandson and many followers continued to teach his ideas.

What he said

❝I hear and I forget, I see and I remember, I do and I understand.❞

Find out more

More about Confucius's life can be found at:
www.crystalinks.com/confucius.html

Find out more about Confucius at:
www.iep.utm.edu/c/confuciu.htm

Read some quotations by Confucius at:
www.quotationspage.com/quotes/Confucius

Timeline

Born in Lu, China

Confucius dies

c. 552 BC   497–484 BC   c. 479 BC   3rd century BC

Travels around China

Analects compiled

Place in history

Confucius's teachings became known as Confucianism. His sayings and conversations can be found in a book called *Analects*. Confucius taught that the way to live a better life was to have good relationships with other people. He gave five **virtues** to follow: kindness, righteousness, sobriety, wisdom, and trustworthiness. Today, there are about five million Confucians in China and East Asia.

Did you know?

Confucius said that you should only treat other people as you would want them to treat you.

35

Laozi

An ancient Chinese philosopher, Laozi was the central figure in the religion of Taoism, which is still practised in East Asia.

What he said

66 The Tao is like a well. It is used but never used up. 99

Did you know?

Some Taoists do exercises called Tai Chi to harmonize the yin and yang forces in their bodies.

Find out more

Thi site explains some of Laozi's influences and his place in Chinese philosophy:
www.iep.utm.edu/l/laozi.htm

This site includes a discussion of Laozi's philosophy and Daoism:
www.hku.hk/philodep/ch/laoency.htm

Laozi's story

Very little is known of Laozi's life. Chinese legend says that he may have lived at around the same time as Confucius (⇨p35). He may have been a scholar and worked for the royal court. Tradition says that he left his job because he disliked the greed and **corruption** of court life. Riding on an ox, he set off to live as a hermit in the mountains. At a mountain pass, he was stopped by a guard who asked him to write down his teachings. This became the *Daodejing*, the sacred text of Taoism.

Timeline

Life of Laozi

The great Tao teacher, Zhuangzi, is born

c. 6th century BC   **4th century BC**   **c. 370 BC**   **3rd century**

Taoism first recognized as a religion

Daodejing compile

Place in history

Laozi taught his followers about the Tao ("Way"), which is the force that connects everything together. The aim of Taoists is to live in harmony with nature. The world is filled with opposing but harmonious forces, such as light and dark, hot and cold, which are thought to be either yin (female) or yang (male). The key to a happy life is to find a balance between yin and yang.

Laozi taught that there were no gods or goddesses, only the Tao. Later, Taoists began to worship many gods in their temples, including Laozi himself.

Qin Shi Huangdi

In 221 BC, Qin Shi Huangdi became the first emperor of China. Under his rule, China was unified as one country for the first time.

Qin Shi Huangdi's story

In the middle of the third century BC, China was divided into many small states, which were constantly at war. In 246 BC, at the age of 13, Qin Shi Huangdi became king of the state of Qin. At first, the kingdom was ruled on his behalf by his mother and the prime minister. Later, Qin Shi Huangdi took over and expanded his kingdom. He was a brilliant soldier and clever **diplomat**. By 221 BC, he had united the states into one kingdom and given himself the title of Shi Huangdi ("first emperor"). Qin Shi Huangdi came up with laws about how to rule his kingdom. His system of government lasted for the next 2,000 years.

What he said

66 From the second generation to the ten thousandth, my line will not end. 99

How did he die?

Qin Shi Huangdi died from swallowing deadly poisonous mercury pills.

Timeline

Qin Shi Huangdi born		Becomes first emperor of China	
c. **259 BC**	**246 BC**	**221 BC**	**210 BC**
	Becomes king of Qin		Qin Shi Huangdi dies

Place in history

Two of Qin Shi Huangdi's greatest achievements can still be seen today. He built the Great Wall of China to protect the northern borders of his empire. The wall is more than 2,400 kilometres (1,491 miles) long and one of the largest structures ever built.

During his lifetime, Qin Shi Huangdi also began building his own tomb. It was like an underground city, guarded by an army of more than 6,000 life-size terracotta (clay) warriors. Buried for centuries, the terracotta army was accidentally rediscovered in 1974 by workmen digging a well.

Find out more

Read an article about the Terracotta Army at:
www.timesonline.co.uk/tol/news/world/asia/china/article2327882.ece

There is even more on the history and politics of Qin Shi Huangdi:
www.thejadetrade.com/ian/p15.html

Find lots of images at the British Museum site:
www.britishmuseum.org

Han Wu Di

Emperor Wu Di was one of the greatest and most powerful emperors of the Han Dynasty in China, ruling from about 141 to 87 BC.

Did you know?

Wu Di was called the Martial Emperor because of his many wars. "Martial" means warlike.

Han Wudi's story

Wu Di was the tenth child of Emperor Jing. He was born with the name Liu Che. When Emperor Jing died in 141 BC, Wu Di became emperor. He was 15 years old. Early on in his rule, Wu Di made everyone follow the ideas of Confucius (⇨p35). He also tried to break away from the control of his grandmother and mother and to make his own decisions on how to govern China.

Find out more

Find out more about Han Wu Di at: www.chinaculture.org/gb/en_aboutchina/ 2003-09/24/content_22864.htm

Another great site: http://china-corner.com/ article_list.asp?id=588

Timeline

Liu Che born

156 BC

141 BC

Becomes Emperor Wu Di

Wu Di dies

87 BC

In around 135 BC, Wu Di began his campaign to further the territories of China. His armies conquered parts of southern China that were outside Han control. Later, Wu Di occupied large parts of Central Asia and southern **Manchuria**.

Place in history

During Emperor Wu Di's long reign, China reached its greatest size. Wu Di also helped to defend China from the **Mongols**. The empire he created was larger than the Roman Empire and one of the greatest in the world. A strong supporter of Confucianism, he was also a ruthless leader, dealing harshly with his enemies.

How did he die?

Emperor Wu Di died aged 69 and was buried in a pyramid-shaped tomb.

Zhang Qian

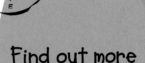

An official in the service of Emperor Wu Di (⇨p38), Zhang Qian was sent on a mission to Central Asia, which brought him lasting fame as an explorer.

About Zhang Qian

In 138 BC, Emperor Wu Di chose Zhang Qian to lead an expedition to Central Asia to find allies against the Xiong-nu people. Although he did not succeed in his mission, Zhang Qian's journey opened up a large stretch of the Silk Road.

Find out more

Read about Zhang Qian's life at:
www.chinaculture.org/gb/
en_aboutchina/2003-09/24/
content_22624.htm

Timeline

Zhang Qian born
Returns to China

195 BC — **138 BC** — **126 BC** — **114 BC**

Leaves China for Central Asia

Zhang Qian dies

Sima Qian

Sima Qian was a famous ancient Chinese historian His work, *Records of the Grand Historian*, tells us about 2,000 years of Chinese history.

About Sima Qian

From a young age, Sima Qian travelled across China, collecting information for his great historical work, *Records of the Grand Historian*. Written in 130 volumes, his work told the history of China from the time of the emperor, Huangdi, in the 26th century BC, to Sima Qian's own day.

Find out more

This site contains extracts from Sima Qian's writing.
www.humanistictexts.org/
simaqian.htm

More about Sima Qian at:
http://journeyeast.tripod.com/
sima_qian.html

Timeline

Sima Qian born
Creates a new calendar

c. 145 BC — **c. 109–91 BC** — **c. 104 BC** — **c. 86 BC**

Compiles the Records

Sima Qian dies

Zhang Heng

A brilliant scholar, Zhang Heng was an astronomer, mathematician, poet, and painter. Among his many achievements, he invented the first seismograph for detecting earthquakes.

What was said

66 The excellence of his talent and the splendour of his art were one with those of the gods. 99

Did you know?

Zhang Heng was a talented poet and one of the greatest painters of his time.

Zhang Heng's story

Born in Nanyang, China, Zhang Heng left home at the age of 16 to study literature. Later, he turned his attention to astronomy, and eventually became chief **astrologer** at the **imperial** court. As part of his work, he mapped the night sky, recording 2,500 stars. He also correctly worked out that the Sun causes the Moon to shine.

Timeline

Born in Nanyang, China

Invents the first seismograph

Dies in Louyang, Ch

AD 78　　**AD 116**　　**AD 132**　　**AD 138**　　**AD 139**

Becomes an official at the imperial court

Seismograph detects an earthquake 800 km (497 miles) away

Find out more

Encyclopaedic entry about this key figure in Chinese history: www.chinaculture.org/gb/en_madeinchina/ 2005-08/18/content_71970.htm

More information about Zhang Heng: www.groups.dcs.st-and.ac.uk/ ~history/Biographies/Zhang_Heng.html

and at: www.cultural-china.com/chinaWH/ html/en/33History159.html

Place in history

Zhang Heng is best remembered for inventing the seismograph. This was particularly important in China, because there are many earthquakes. The seismograph was a large bronze vase. Around the side of the vase were dragons' heads. Each dragon held a ball. Below each dragon was a toad. During an earthquake, a pendulum tilted inside the vase and swung towards a dragon. The dragon then dropped its ball into the toad's mouth. This recorded the direction of the earthquake waves. Zhang named his new invention Di Dong Yi, or "Earth Motion Instrument".

Pakal the Great

Pakal the Great was the ruler of the ancient Maya city of Palenque in Mexico in the 7th century. Pakal was a great ruler who rebuilt his city after a war.

Pakal's story

Pakal was born in around 603 and became ruler of Palenque at the age of 12. He succeeded his mother. It is thought that he married a princess and had two sons. During Pakal's rule, Palenque was rebuilt after being damaged in attacks by a rival city. Pakal ordered new palaces and temples to be built, and the city became very powerful. Some of the finest art and architecture of Maya times came during Pakal's rule.

What was said about the tomb

" Out of the dim shadows emerged a vision from a fairy tale, a fantastic sight from another world. "

Timeline

Born in Palenque		Gets married		
c. 603	615	624		683
	Becomes ruler of Palenque			Dies in Palenque

Find out more

Read about Pakal the Great at: www.mesoweb.com/palenque/features/ sarcophagus/pakals_tomb.html

This site has some useful information about Palenque: www.delange.org/PalenqueRuins/ PalenqueRuins.htm

Pakal was succeeded by his eldest son who continued the work begun by his father. He also completed his father's famous tomb.

Place in history

Pakal the Great is best known for his remarkable tomb. While **excavating** the ruins of the Temple of Inscriptions in Palenque in the 1950s, Mexican archaeologist, Alberto Ruz, discovered a huge room deep inside. It contained a large stone slab. Beneath the slab lay a tomb containing the skeleton of Pakal the Great. Covering Pakal's face was an exquisite death mask made from hundreds of pieces of the precious stone, jade. It was one of the most amazing finds in Maya archaeology.

How did he die?

Pakal the Great died at the age of 80. After his death he was worshipped as a god.

Jasaw

Jasaw Chan K'awiil I, also known as Ruler A, was the ruler of the great Maya city of Tikal in Guatemala in the late 7th and early 8th centuries. His tomb is the famous Temple of the Great Jaguar (see left).

About Jasaw

Find out more

Find out more about Jasaw at: www.utexas.edu/cofa/a_ah/dir/precol/maya_tikal.html

During Jasaw's reign, Tikal became powerful and prosperous. Jasaw built many spectacular temples. At the base of the Temple of the Great Jaguar is Jasaw's tomb. His skeleton was found lying on the remains of a woven mat.

Timeline

	Defeats the rival city of Calakmul		Jasaw dies
c. 682	c. 695	c. 704	c. 734
Becomes ruler of Tikal		Jasaw's wife dies	

Eighteen Rabbit

Eighteen Rabbit was the nickname of Uaxaclajuun Ub'aah K'awiil. He was the 13th ruler of the Mayan city of Copan in Honduras.

About Eighteen Rabbit

Find out more

Find out more about the ruins at Copan: www.vivatravelguides.com/central-america/honduras/honduras-articles/copan-ruins/

In around AD 739, Copan suffered a terrible defeat at the hands of a rival city. Copan's ruler, Eighteen Rabbit, was captured and beheaded, and a new ruler, nicknamed Smoke Monkey, took over. Today, the impressive ruins at Copan are protected.

Timeline

Becomes ruler of Copan		Eighteen Rabbit dies
c. 695	c. 731	c. 738
	Copan becomes powerful	

Acamapichtli

The first tlatoani (ruler) of the Aztecs,
Acamapichtli reigned from 1376 to 1395.
He was the founder of the Aztec Empire.

Acamapichtli's story

In around 1325 or 1345, the Aztecs began to build their
great capital. This was an island called Tenochtitlan in the
middle of Lake Texcoco in the Valley of Mexico. Their
leader at that time was called Tenoch. When Tenoch died
in about 1375, the Aztecs chose Acamapichtli to succeed
him. He began his rule as governor and lived in the nearby
city of Texcoco. Later, he moved to Tenochtitlan and was
crowned tlatoani (ruler) in 1382. His elaborate **coronation**
ceremony was followed by all the later Aztec rulers.

Did you know?

The tlatoani was
so important that
ordinary people were
not allowed to look
at him.

Timeline

Founding of Tenochtitlan		Becomes ruler of the Aztecs		Acamapichtli dies
1325 or 1345	c. 1375	1376	1382	1395
	Tenoch dies		Crowned tlatoani	

Place in history

During Acamapichtli's rule, Tenochtitlan grew in
size and power. Acamapichtli was a good politician.
He made friends with neighbouring rulers and lived
in a time of peace. Tenochtitlan was made
bigger by rock and soil from the mainland.
The new land was used to make chinampas
(floating gardens) on which the Aztecs grew
maize and other crops. Acamapichtli also divided
the city into four zones and built a great temple.

Before his death, Acamapichtli called the chiefs
of Tenochtitlan together to choose his successor.
They elected his eldest son, Huitzilihuitl.

Find out more

Find out more information
about Acamapichtli at:
www.freewebs.com/tecpaocelotl/
MexicaTlahtoani.htm

An excellent site about the Aztecs:
http://home.freeuk.net/elloughton13/
mexico.htm

Itzcoatl

The fourth Aztec ruler, Itzcoatl was the son of Acamapichtli (⇨p43). During his rule, the Aztecs defeated their arch enemies.

About Itzcoatl

For a while, the Aztec capital Tenochtitlan was taken over by the Tepanecs. The Tepanecs lived on the west shore of Lake Texcoco. At the time, Itzcoatl was the Aztec tlatoani (ruler). He defeated the Tepanecs. He was helped by the rulers of the nearby cities of Texcoco and Tlacopan.

Find out more

Find out more about Itzcoatl at:
www.brownpride.com/history/history.asp?a=aztecs/emperors

Timeline

Founding of Tenochtitlan	Reign of Acamapichtli	Becomes tlatoani	Itzcoatl dies
1325 or 1345	c. 1376–1395	c. 1427 or 1428	c. 1440

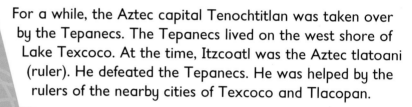

Ahuitzotl

Ahuitzotl was the eighth Aztec tlatoani (ruler) and a great military leader. After taking power, he set about expanding Aztec territories and strengthening the empire.

About Ahuitzotl

Ahuitzotl led his army on long campaigns and expanded the empire to twice its previous size. Ahuitzotl also began a major rebuilding of the city of Tenochtitlan. This included the Great Temple, which was dedicated to Huitzilopochtli, god of war and the sun.

Find out more

Read more about the life and times of Ahuitzotl:
www.ancientworlds.net/aw/Post/912070

Timeline

Becomes tlatoani	Rebuilds the Great Temple	Ahuitzotl dies
c. 1486	c. 1487	c. 1502

Moctezuma II

Moctezuma II was the Aztec tlatoani in the early 16th century. He was the ruler when Spanish explorers invaded Mexico.

Moctezuma's story

Moctezuma became ruler in around 1502. During his reign, he waged war on many of his neighbours and seized their lands. With these conquests, the Aztec Empire reached its greatest size. Moctezuma ruled over 5 million people.

In April 1519, however, Spanish invaders landed on the Mexican coast. They were led by Hernán Cortés. Their mission was to claim land for Spain, but they were also greedy and wanted Aztec gold.

What he said

66 It was fated that I should be cast from the throne of my ancestors and leave it in ruins. 99

How did he die?

Moctezuma II may have been killed by his own people.

Timeline

Moctezuma II born		Spanish enter Tenochtitlan		Siege of Tenochtitlan
c. **1466**	c. **1502**	**1519**	**1520**	**1521**
	Becomes tlatoani		Moctezuma II dies	

Place in history

Eventually, Cortés reached Tenochtitlan. Moctezuma greeted him warmly, believing him to be a god. Cortés led his army into the city, and then left to fetch allies. While he was gone, the friendship between the Aztecs and Spanish broke down. Cortés returned and took Moctezuma prisoner. Moctezuma later died.

In 1521, Cortés forced the Aztecs to surrender. Within two years of Cortés's return, Tenochtitlan's riches had been stolen and the Aztec Empire lay in ruins.

Find out more

Find out how Moctezuma II ruled his empire at:
www.cartage.org.lb/en/themes/
Biographies/MainBiographies/
M/Montezuma/a72.html

This site has different descriptions and reports about Moctezuma's appearance:
www.reportret.info/gallery/
motecuhzoma1.html

Read more about Moctezuma II:
www.mexconnect.com/mex_/history/
jtuck/jtmoctezuma2.html

Glossary

archaeologist A person who studies history by digging up ancient objects and buildings from the past.

architect A person who designs buildings and supervizes their construction.

assassinated When an important political figure is murdered.

Assyria The northern part of Mesopotamia.

astrologer A person who studies how the stars and planets may affect people's lives.

banished Sent away from a place as a form of punishment.

besieged When a place is surrounded by an army to bring about its surrender.

civil war A war between two sides from the same country.

coronation The ceremony held when a king, queen or emperor is crowned.

corruption An act of dishonesty.

democratic A political system in which all citizens have a say.

dictator An important government official in Ancient Rome.

diplomat A person who tries to solve problems on behalf of a government.

dynasty A family of rulers who pass on the throne through the generations.

emperor The ruler of an empire.

empire A group of people and land ruled over by an emperor.

epic A long poem telling the story of a heroic figure.

excavating Digging up ancient objects from the past.

exiled When a person is banished from his or her homeland..

immortal Not likely to die. Gods and goddesses were believed to be immortal.

imperial Connected to an empire or emperor.

improvident Unwise or careless.

Manchuria A region of ancient north-east China.

Medea In ancient times, a region of north-west Iran.

Mesopotamia The ancient name for the land between the Rivers Tigris and Euphrates, which lies mostly in modern-day Iraq.

Mongols Warriors from Mongolia who conquered a vast empire in the 12th century.

mortal Human beings and other living things that can die.

mummy A body that has been wrapped in bandages ready for burial.

pharaoh The title given to the ruler of Ancient Egypt.

philosopher A scholar in Ancient Greece who studied all aspects of the world around them.

Phoenicia A place in the eastern Mediterranean (modern-day Lebanon) from around 1200 BC.

provinces Regions of the Roman Empire outside Italy ruled by governors from Rome.

regent Someone who rules in the place of the actual ruler.

republic A country or state which is governed by elected representatives of the people, rather than a king or emperor.

senators The group of officials that governed Ancient Rome.

scribe A person specially trained in reading and writing.

Sumer The southern part of Mesopotamia.

virtues Good qualities.

Index